Oxford Very First Dictionary

Compiled by Clare Kirtley
Illustrated by Georgie Birkett

OXFORD
UNIVERSITY PRESS

Oxford
Very First
Dictionary

'For Rose, Amy and Eleanor' – C.K.

OXFORD
UNIVERSITY PRESS

Great Clarendon Street, Oxford OX2 6DP

Oxford University Press is a department of the University of Oxford.
It furthers the University's objective of excellence in research, scholarship,
and education by publishing worldwide in

Oxford   New York
Auckland   Cape Town   Dar es Salaam   Hong Kong   Karachi
Kuala Lumpur   Madrid   Melbourne   Mexico City   Nairobi
New Delhi   Shanghai   Taipei   Toronto

With offices in

Argentina Austria Brazil Chile Czech Republic France Greece
Guatemala Hungary Italy Japan Poland Portugal Singapore
South Korea Switzerland Thailand Turkey Ukraine Vietnam

© Oxford University Press 2007

Database right Oxford University Press (maker)

First published in 1999 as My Very First Oxford Dictionary
Reissued in 2003 as Oxford Very First Dictionary
Reissued in 2007

British Library Cataloguing in Publication Data
Data available

ISBN 9780-19-9115419 (hardback)
ISBN 9780-19-9115426 (paperback)
ISBN 9780-19-9117758 (Big Book)

1 3 5 7 9 10 8 6 4 2

Printed in Singapore by KHL Printing Co. Pte Ltd. (hardback and paperback)
Printed in China (Big Book)

Contents

Introduction

The **Oxford Very First Dictionary** helps young children enjoy and discover the features of a dictionary. It contains over 300 words in alphabetical order, each with a simple definition and a colourful picture. There are also additional end sections with words that children will find useful when writing. The words have been chosen to support and develop speaking, reading, and writing.

Here are the main features on the **A** to **Z** pages:

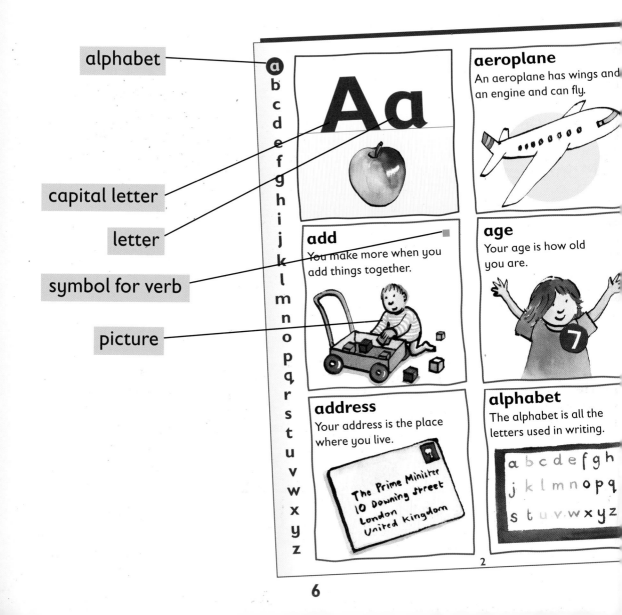

alphabet

capital letter

letter

symbol for verb

picture

aeroplane
An aeroplane has wings and an engine and can fly.

add
You make more when you add things together.

age
Your age is how old you are.

address
Your address is the place where you live.

The Prime Minister
10 Downing Street
London
United Kingdom

alphabet
The alphabet is all the letters used in writing.

a b c d e f g h
j k l m n o p q
s t u v w x y z

2

The **Oxford Very First Dictionary** is an ideal introduction to dictionaries and other alphabetically ordered reference books. It helps children acquire basic dictionary and reference skills in a simple and enjoyable way: they can learn about the alphabet and about alphabetical order; they can find out how to locate a word by using the initial letter; they can check their own spelling; and they can learn how to use simple definitions of words.

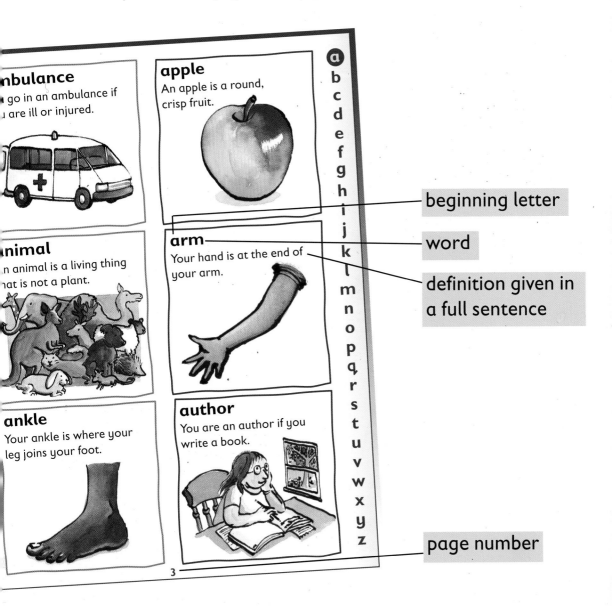

mbulance
go in an ambulance if
u are ill or injured.

apple
An apple is a round, crisp fruit.

nimal
n animal is a living thing
hat is not a plant.

arm
Your hand is at the end of
your arm.

ankle
Your ankle is where your
leg joins your foot.

author
You are an author if you
write a book.

a b c d e f g h i j k l m n o p q r s t u v w x y z

3

beginning letter

word

definition given in a full sentence

page number

Aa

aeroplane

An aeroplane has wings and an engine and can fly.

add

You make more when you add things together.

age

Your age is how old you are.

address

Your address is the place where you live.

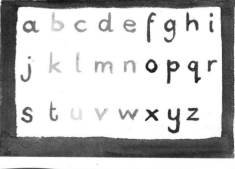

The Prime Minister
10 Downing Street
London
United Kingdom

alphabet

The alphabet is all the letters used in writing.

a b c d e f g h i
j k l m n o p q r
s t u v w x y z

ambulance

You go in an ambulance if you are ill or injured.

apple

An apple is a round, crisp fruit.

animal

An animal is a living thing that is not a plant.

arm

Your hand is at the end of your arm.

ankle

Your ankle is where your leg joins your foot.

author

You are an author if you write a book.

Bb

bear

A bear is a big furry animal.

ball

A ball is round. You can play games with it.

bed

You sleep in a bed.

banana

A banana is a long yellow fruit.

bicycle

A bicycle has two wheels. You ride a bicycle.

big

If something is big it is large.

bounce

A ball comes back up again when you bounce it.

bird

A bird has wings, feathers and a beak.

bread

You make bread with flour and bake it in the oven.

book

A book has pages and a cover.

bus

A bus can carry lots of people.

Cc

car

A car has wheels and an engine.

cake

A cake is a sweet food.

cat

A cat is a small furry animal.

camera

You take photos with a camera.

chair

You sit on a chair.

cheese

You make cheese from milk.

cook

You cook food by heating it.

clock

A clock tells you the time.

cow

A cow is a farm animal that gives milk.

computer

A computer stores information.

cup

You drink things from a cup.

a b **c** d e f g h i j k l m n o p q r s t u v w x y z

Dd

day

It is light during the day.

dance

You move to music when you dance.

dinosaur

A dinosaur is an animal that lived a long time ago.

date

A date is the day something happens.

MONDAY
5
MARCH

doctor

A doctor makes you better if you are ill.

dog

You can keep a dog as a pet.

dress

A girl sometimes wears a dress.

doll

A doll is a toy person.

drink

You can drink milk.

door

You open a door to go into a room.

duck

A duck is a bird that likes water.

a b c **d** e f g h i j k l m n o p q r s t u v w x y z

Ee

eat

You need to eat food to live.

ear

You use your ears to hear.

egg

A bird lives inside an egg before it is born.

earth

You live on the planet Earth.

elbow

You bend your arm at your elbow.

electricity

You use electricity to get light and heat.

envelope

You put a letter in an envelope.

elephant

An elephant has a long nose called a trunk.

exercise

You need to exercise to keep fit.

empty

If something is empty it has nothing in it.

eye

You use your eyes to see.

Ff

farm

A farm is where food is grown.

fairy

You can read about a fairy in stories.

feather

Birds have feathers instead of fur or hair.

fall

You come down quickly when you fall.

fish

A fish lives under water.

flower

A flower is part of a plant.

fox

A fox is a wild animal with a furry tail.

foot

Your foot is at the end of your leg.

frog

A frog has wet skin and webbed feet.

fork

You use a fork to eat.

fruit

You can eat fruit. Apples and oranges are fruit.

Gg

garden
You can grow flowers and vegetables in a garden.

game
You play a game.

gate
A gate is an outside door.

garage
A car is kept in a garage.

giant
A giant is a very big person.

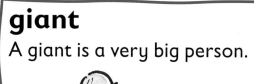

giraffe
A giraffe has a long neck.

good
If something is good you like it.

glass
A window is made of glass.

grow
Things get bigger when they grow.

glue
You use glue to stick things together.

guitar
A guitar is an instrument with strings.

a b c d e f **g** h i j k l m n o p q r s t u v w x y z

21

Hh

head

Your eyes and ears are on your head.

hand

You hold things with your hand.

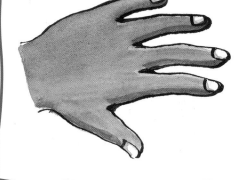

helicopter

A helicopter has blades that spin round on top.

hat

You wear a hat on your head.

hill

A hill is a piece of high land.

holiday

A holiday is when you do not go to school or work.

hot

If something is hot it can burn you.

horse

You can ride a horse.

house

You can live in a house.

hospital

You go to hospital if you are ill.

hungry

If you are hungry you want to eat.

a b c d e f g h i j k l m n o p q r s t u v w x y z

Ii

information

You use information to find out about things.

ice

Freezing water turns to ice.

insect

An insect is a small animal with six legs.

ill

If you are ill you do not feel well.

instrument

You use an instrument to make music.

Jj

jug
You use a jug to pour a drink.

jam
You make jam from fruit and sugar.

juggler
A juggler throws things up and catches them.

journey
You travel from place to place on a journey.

jump
You go up into the air when you jump.

a b c d e f g h i **j** k l m n o p q r s t u v w x y z

Kk

kettle

You use a kettle to boil water.

kangaroo

A kangaroo has big back legs and jumps.

key

You use a key to unlock a door.

keep

If you keep something you do not give it away.

kick

You kick a ball with your foot.

kind

You are being kind when you help other people.

kite

A kite flies in the air at the end of a long string.

king

Some countries are ruled by a king.

knee

Your knee is where your leg bends.

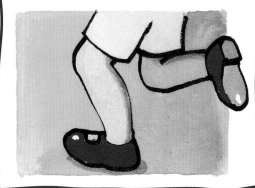

kitchen

You cook in a kitchen.

knife

You use a knife to cut things.

a b c d e f g h i j **k** l m n o p q r s t u v w x y z

Ll

leaf

A leaf grows on a plant.

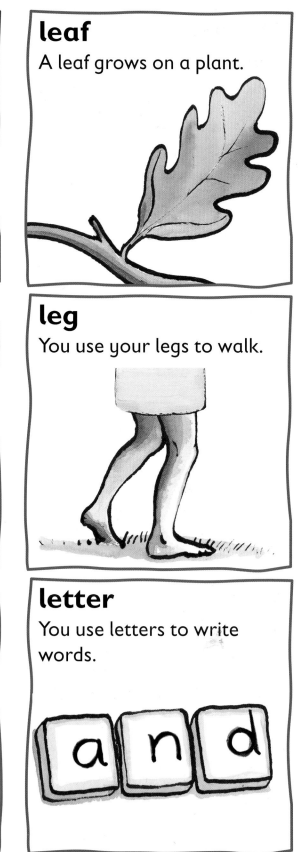

ladybird

A ladybird is a small flying insect with spots.

leg

You use your legs to walk.

laugh

You laugh when something is funny.

letter

You use letters to write words.

library
Books are kept in a library.

little
If something is little it is not big.

like
If you like someone you think they are nice.

look
You use your eyes to look.

lion
A lion is a big wild cat.

loud
You can hear loud sounds easily.

Mm

meat
We eat meat from animals.

make
You make something by putting things together.

metal
Something made of metal is hard.

map
A map shows you how to get to places.

microwave
A microwave oven cooks food quickly.

a b c d e f g h i j k l m n o p q r s t u v w x y z

milk
You can drink cow's milk.

moon
You often see the moon in the sky at night.

money
You use money to buy things.

mountain
A mountain is a high hill.

monkey
A monkey is furry and lives in trees.

mouth
You use your mouth to speak and eat.

a b c d e f g h i j k l **m** n o p q r s t u v w x y z

Nn

necklace

You wear a necklace around your neck.

name

Your name is what people call you.

nest

A bird lives in a nest.

neck

Your neck joins your head to your shoulders.

new

Something is new when you first get it.

nice

If something is nice you enjoy it.

nose

You use your nose to smell.

night

It is dark at night time.

number

You use numbers to count.

noise

A noise is a loud sound.

nurse

A nurse looks after you when you are ill.

a b c d e f g h i j k l m **n** o p q r s t u v w x y z

Oo

open

You can open a door.

octopus

An octopus has eight arms.

orange

An orange is a round fruit with thick peel.

old

You are old if you were born a long time ago.

owl

An owl is a bird who flies at night.

Pp

park
You can play in a park.

page
A page is part of a book.

pencil
You use a pencil to write or draw.

paper
You write on paper.

piano
A piano is an instrument with black and white keys.

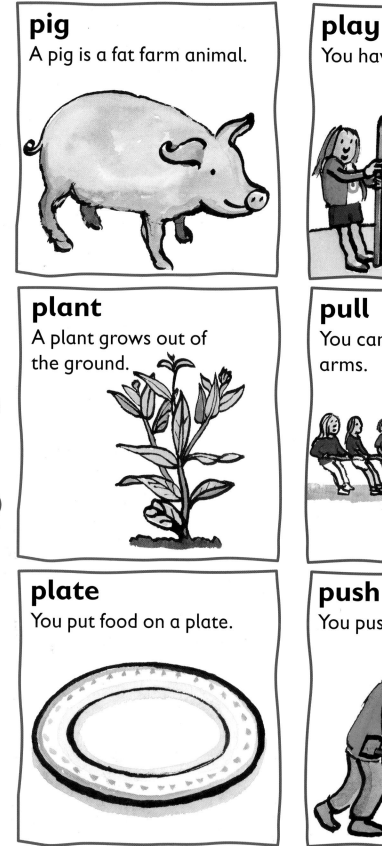

pig
A pig is a fat farm animal.

play
You have fun when you play.

plant
A plant grows out of the ground.

pull
You can pull with your arms.

plate
You put food on a plate.

push
You push a wheelbarrow.

Qq

queue

You line up in a queue to wait for a bus.

queen

A queen is a woman who rules a country.

quick

You are quick when you move fast.

question

You ask a question to find out something.

quiet

You are quiet when you make very little noise.

Rr

rainbow

Sun shines through rain to make a rainbow.

rabbit

A rabbit is a small animal with long ears.

read

You read books, cards and letters.

rain

The rain is water falling from the sky.

recorder

A recorder is an instrument that you blow.

rhinoceros

A rhinoceros has a horn on its nose.

robot

A robot is a machine that moves like a person.

river

A river is a large stream of water.

rocket

A rocket sends spacecraft into space.

road

Cars and buses travel on a road.

run

You move your legs quickly to run.

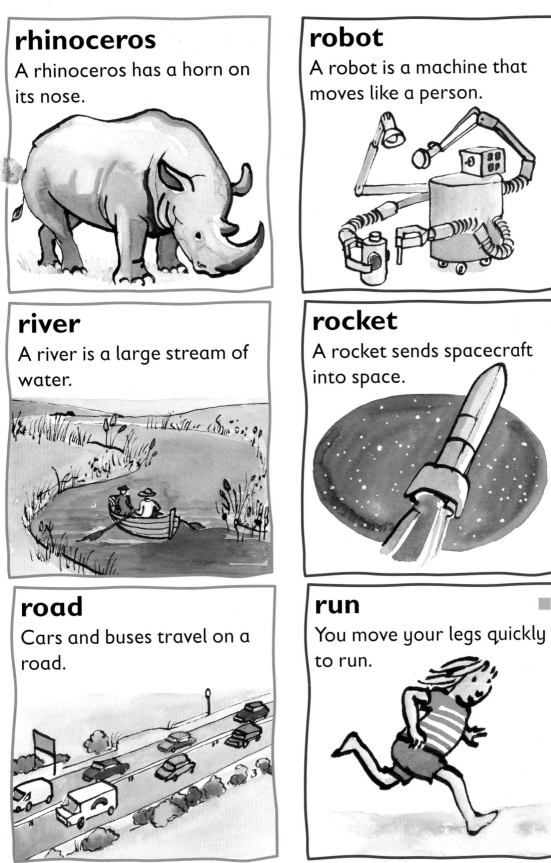

a b c d e f g h i j k l m n o p q r s t u v w x y z

Ss

seed

A plant grows from a seed.

school

You go to school to learn.

sheep

You get wool from a sheep.

scissors

You use scissors to cut things.

shirt

A shirt has sleeves and a collar.

shoe
You wear a shoe on your foot.

sock
You wear a sock on your foot.

shop
You buy things in a shop.

story
A story tells you about something that has happened.

snow
Snow falls when it is very cold.

sun
It is warm and bright in the sun.

a b c d e f g h i j k l m n o p q r **s** t u v w x y z

Tt

teeth
You use your teeth to bite.

table
You sit at a table.

telephone
You use a telephone to speak to people.

teacher
A teacher helps you to learn.

television
You watch and listen to things on television.

towel

You use a towel to dry yourself.

train

A train goes on a track.

town

There are lots of buildings in a town.

tree

A tree is a tall plant with leaves.

toy

You play with a toy.

trousers

You wear trousers on your legs.

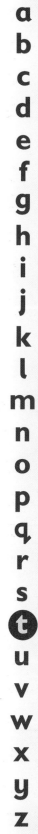

Uu

uniform
The police and nurses wear a uniform.

ugly
If something is ugly it is not nice to look at.

upset
You are not happy when you are upset.

umbrella
You use an umbrella to keep dry when it rains.

use
You use tools to make things.

Vv

vegetable

A vegetable is a plant that you can eat.

van

A van can carry lots of things.

video

A video records sound and pictures from the television.

vase

You put flowers in a vase.

violin

You play a violin with a bow.

a b c d e f g h i j k l m n o p q r s t u **v** w x y z

W w

wind

The wind is air moving.

wall

A wall is made of brick or stone.

word

You use words when you speak or write.

dog
chair
bed
hat

water

Rivers and seas are made up of water.

write

You write words for other people to read.

write
w

Xx

Yy

X-ray
An X-ray shows the inside of your body.

yacht
A yacht is a boat with sails.

xylophone
A xylophone is an instrument with wooden bars.

yawn
You yawn when you are tired.

a b c d e f g h i j k l m n o p q r s t u v w **x** **y** z

year

There are twelve months in a year.

JULY

Zz

yogurt

You make yogurt from sour milk.

zebra

A zebra has black and white stripes.

young

You are young if you were born a short time ago.

zigzag

A zigzag line turns sharply.

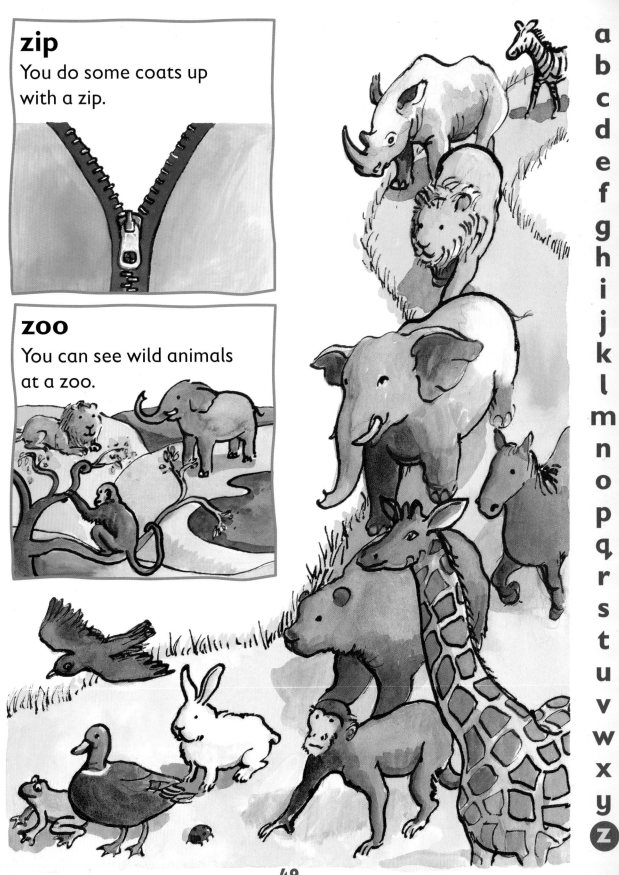

zip
You do some coats up with a zip.

zoo
You can see wild animals at a zoo.

a b c d e f g h i j k l m n o p q r s t u v w x y z

49

Words we write a lot

a
about
after
again
all
am
an
and
another
are
as
at
away

back
ball
be
because
bed
been
big
boy
brother
but
by

call
called
came
can
can't
cat
children
come
could
cross

dad
day
did
dig
do
dog
don't
door
down

end
every
everyone

first
for
from

get
girl
go
going
good
got

had
half
has
have
he
help
her
here
him
his
home
house
how

I
if
in
is
it

jump
just

last
laugh
like
liked
little
live
lived
look
looked
lots
love

made
make
man
many
may
me
more
much
mum
must
my

name
new
next
night
no
not
now

said
saw
school
see
seen
she
should
sister
sit
so
some

under
up
us

very

of
off
old
on
once
one
or
our
out
over

want
was
water
way
we
went
were
what
when
where
who
why
will
with
would

people
play
please
pull
pulled
push
put

take
than
thank
that
the
their
them
then
there
these
they
this
three
time
to
too
took
tree
two

yes
you
your

ran

Verbs (These are doing words)

add

carry

cry

catch

clap

climb

cut

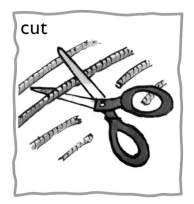

dance

bounce

buy

call

cook

dig

drink

grow

keep

eat

hear

kick

help

exercise

laugh

hop

fall

jump

like

More verbs

listen

paint

run

look

play

see

pull

make

sing

push

open

read

sit

sleep

talk

walk

smell

taste

wash

smile

throw

write

write

take

touch

use

yawn

Colours

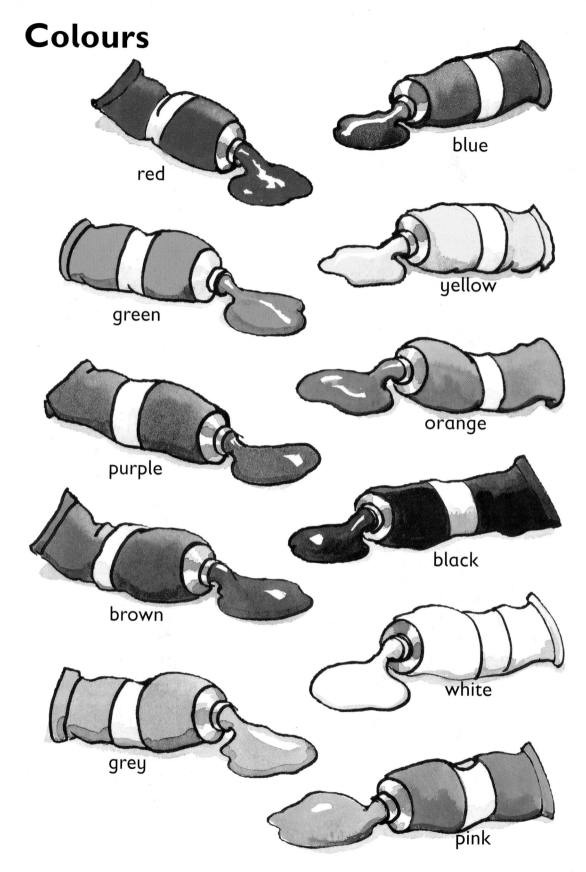

red

blue

green

yellow

purple

orange

brown

black

grey

white

pink

Shapes

square

triangle

circle

rectangle

Days of the week

Sunday

Monday

Saturday

Tuesday

Friday

Wednesday

Thursday

Months of the year

January

July

February

August

March

September

April

October

May

November

June

December

Numbers

zero	**0**	
one	1	
two	**2**	
three	3	
four	4	
five	**5**	
six	6	
seven	**7**	
eight	8	
nine	**9**	

ten	**10**	
eleven	**11**	
twelve	12	
thirteen	**13**	
fourteen	**14**	
fifteen	15	
sixteen	**16**	
seventeen	**17**	
eighteen	**18**	
nineteen	19	
twenty	**20**	

The alphabet

A a

B b

C c

D d

E e

F f

G g

H h

I i

J j

K k

L l

Mm  Tt

Nn

Uu

Oo

Vv

Pp

Ww

Qq

Xx

Rr

Yy

Ss

Zz